CIMA

How to access your on-line resources

Kaplan Financial students will have a MyKaplan account and these extra resources will be available to you online. You do not need to register again, as this process was completed when you enrolled. If you are having problems accessing online materials, please ask your course administrator.

If you are not studying with Kaplan and did not purchase your book via a Kaplan website, to unlock your extra online resources please go to www.en-gage.co.uk (even if you have set up an account and registered books previously). You will then need to enter the ISBN number (on the title page and back cover) and the unique pass key number contained in the scratch panel below to gain access.

You will also be required to enter additional information during this process to set up or confirm your account details.

If you purchased via the Kaplan Publishing website you will automatically receive an e-mail invitation to register your details and gain access to your content. If you do not receive the e-mail or book content, please contact Kaplan Publishing.

Your code and information

This code can only be used once for the registration of one book online. This registration and your online content will expire when the final sittings for the examinations covered by this book have taken place. Please allow one hour from the time you submit your book details for us to process your request.

Please scratch the film to access your unique code.

KAPLAN

PUBLISHING

Operational Level

Subject E1

Managing Finance in a Digital World

EXAM PRACTICE KIT

British Library Cataloguing-in-Publication Data

A catalogue record for this book is available from the British Library.

Published by:

Kaplan Publishing UK
Unit 2 The Business Centre
Molly Millar's Lane
Wokingham
Berkshire
RG41 2QZ

ISBN: 978-1-78740-205-8

© Kaplan Financial Limited, 2019

CONTENTS

Section

Quality and accuracy are of the utmost importance to us so if you spot an error in any of our products, please send an email to mykaplanreporting@kaplan.com with full details.

Our Quality Co-ordinator will work with our technical team to verify the error and take action to ensure it is corrected in future editions.

INDEX TO QUESTIONS AND ANSWERS

OBJECTIVE TEST QUESTIONS

EXAM TECHNIQUES

COMPUTER-BASED ASSESSMENT

Golden rules

1   Make sure you have completed the compulsory 15-minute tutorial before you start the test. This tutorial is available through the CIMA website and focusses on the functionality of the exam. You cannot speak to the invigilator once you have started.

2   These exam practice kits give you plenty of exam style questions to practise so make sure you use them to fully prepare.

3   Attempt all questions, there is no negative marking.

4   Double check your answer before you put in the final answer although you can change your response as many times as you like.

5   Not all questions will be multiple choice questions (MCQs) – you may have to fill in missing words or figures.

6   Identify the easy questions first and get some points on the board to build up your confidence.

7   Attempt 'wordy' questions first as these may be quicker than the computation style questions. This will relieve some of the time pressure you will be under during the exam.

8   If you don't know the answer, flag the question and attempt it later. In your final review before the end of the exam try a process of elimination.

9   Work out your answer on the whiteboard provided first if it is easier for you. There is also an onscreen 'scratch pad' on which you can make notes. You are not allowed to take pens, pencils, rulers, pencil cases, phones, paper or notes into the testing room.

SYLLABUS GUIDANCE, LEARNING OBJECTIVES AND VERBS

A   CIMA 2019 PROFESSIONAL QUALIFICATION

Details regarding the content of the CIMA 2019 professional qualification can be located within the CIMA 2019 professional qualification syllabus document.

You can use the following diagram showing the whole structure of your qualification to help you keep track of your progress. Make sure you carefully review the 2019 CIMA syllabus transition rules and seek appropriate advice if you are unsure about your progression through the qualification.

Reproduced with permission from CIMA

B   STUDY WEIGHTINGS

Each Objective Test comprises 60 questions drawn from across individual subjects of the syllabus in line with the weightings for each content area as set out in the blueprint.

C   LEARNING OUTCOMES

Each subject within the qualification is divided into a number of broad syllabus topics. The topics contain one or more lead learning outcomes, related component learning outcomes and indicative knowledge content.

A learning outcome has two main purposes:

1   to define the skill or ability that a well-prepared candidate should be able to exhibit in the examination

2   to demonstrate the approach likely to be taken by examiners in examination questions.

The learning outcomes are part of a hierarchy of learning objectives. The verbs used at the beginning of each learning outcome relate to a specific learning objective, e.g. understand how data is collected, cleaned and connected by finance.

The verb 'understand' indicates a low-level learning objective (level 1/2). As learning objectives are hierarchical, it is expected that at this level students will be able to comprehend ideas, concepts and techniques with regards to how data is collected, cleaned and connected by finance.

The examination blueprints and representative task statements

CIMA have also published examination blueprints giving learners clear expectations regarding what is expected of them. This can be accessed here www.cimaglobal.com/examblueprints

The blueprint is structured as follows:

* Exam content sections (reflecting the syllabus document)

* Lead and component outcomes (reflecting the syllabus document)

* Representative task statements.

A representative task statement is a plain English description of what a CIMA finance professional should know and be able to do.

The content and skill level determine the language and verbs used in the representative task.

CIMA will test up to the level of the task statement in the objective test (an objective test question on a particular topic could be set at a lower level than the task statement in the blueprint).

The format of the objective test blueprints follows that of the published syllabus for the 2019 CIMA Professional Qualification.

Weightings for content sections are also included in the individual subject blueprints.

A list of the learning objectives and the verbs that appear in the syllabus learning outcomes and examinations follows and these will help you to understand the depth and breadth required for a topic and the skill level the topic relates to.

CIMA verb hierarchy

Skill level	Verbs used	Definition
Level 5 **Evaluation** How you are expected to use your learning to evaluate, make decisions or recommendations	Advise	Counsel, inform or notify
	Assess	Evaluate or estimate the nature, ability or quality of
	Evaluate	Appraise or assess the value of
	Recommend	Propose a course of action
	Review	Assess and evaluate in order, to change if necessary
Level 4 **Analysis** How you are expected to analyse the detail of what you have learned	Align	Arrange in an orderly way
	Analyse	Examine in detail the structure of
	Communicate	Share or exchange information
	Compare and contrast	Show the similarities and/or differences between
	Develop	Grow and expand a concept
	Discuss	Examine in detail by argument
	Examine	Inspect thoroughly
	Interpret	Translate into intelligible or familiar terms
	Monitor	Observe and check the progress of
	Prioritise	Place in order of priority or sequence for action
	Produce	Create or bring into existence
Level 3 **Application** How you are expected to apply your knowledge	Apply	Put to practical use
	Calculate	Ascertain or reckon mathematically
	Conduct	Organise and carry out
	Demonstrate	Prove with certainty or exhibit by practical means
	Prepare	Make or get ready for use
	Reconcile	Make or prove consistent/compatible
Level 2 **Comprehension** What you are expected to understand	Describe	Communicate the key features of
	Distinguish	Highlight the differences between
	Explain	Make clear or intelligible/state the meaning or purpose of
	Identify	Recognise, establish or select after consideration
	Illustrate	Use an example to describe or explain something
Level 1 **Knowledge** What you are expected to know	List	Make a list of
	State	Express, fully or clearly, the details/facts of
	Define	Give the exact meaning of
	Outline	Give a summary of

D   OBJECTIVE TEST

Objective test

Objective test questions require you to choose or provide a response to a question whose correct answer is predetermined.

The most common types of objective test question you will see are:

- Multiple choice, where you have to choose the correct answer(s) from a list of possible answers. This could either be numbers or text.

- Multiple response, for example, choosing two correct answers from a list of eight possible answers. This could either be numbers or text.

- Fill in the blank (numerical answers only), where you fill in your answer within the provided space.

- Drag and drop, for example, matching a technical term with the correct definition.

- Hot spots, where you select an answer by clicking on graphs/diagrams.

Guidance re CIMA on-screen calculator

As part of the CIMA objective test software, candidates are now provided with a calculator. This calculator is on-screen and is available for the duration of the assessment. The calculator is available in each of the objective tests and is accessed by clicking the calculator button in the top left hand corner of the screen at any time during the assessment. Candidates are permitted to utilise personal calculators as long as they are an approved CIMA model. CIMA approved model list is found here: https://www.cimaglobal.com/Studying/study-and-resources/.

All candidates must complete a 15-minute exam tutorial before the assessment begins and will have the opportunity to familiarise themselves with the calculator and practise using it. The exam tutorial is also available online via the CIMA website. Candidates can use their own calculators providing it is included in CIMA's authorised calculator listing.

Fundamentals of objective tests

The objective tests are 90-minute assessments comprising 60 compulsory questions, with one or more parts. There will be no choice and all questions should be attempted. All elements of a question must be answered correctly for the question to be marked correctly. All questions are equally weighted.

APPROACH TO REVISION

Stage 1: Assess areas of strengths and weaknesses

Stage 2: Question practice

Follow the order of revision of topics as recommended in the revision table plan below and attempt the questions in the order suggested.

Try to avoid referring to text books and notes and the model answer until you have completed your attempt.

Try to answer the question in the allotted time.

Review your attempt with the model answer and assess how much of the answer you achieved in the allocated exam time.

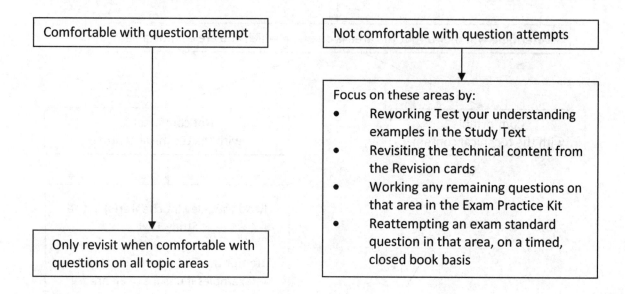

Stage 3: Final pre-exam revision

We recommend that you **attempt at least one ninety minute mock examination** containing a set of previously unseen exam standard questions.

It is important that you get a feel for the breadth of coverage of a real exam without advanced knowledge of the topic areas covered – just as you will expect to see on the real exam day.

Ideally a mock examination offered by your tuition provider should be sat in timed, closed book, real exam conditions.

Information concerning formulae and tables will be provided via the CIMA website: www.cimaglobal.com.

SYLLABUS GRIDS

E1: Managing Finance in a Digital World

How the finance function is organised

Content weighting

Content area	Weighting
A Role of the Finance Function	20%
B Technology in a Digital World	20%
C Data and Information in a Digital World	20%
D Shape and Structure of the Finance Function	20%
E Finance Interacting with the Organisation	20%
	100%

E1A: Role of the Finance Function

This section examines the roles that finance plays in organisations and why. It describes in detail the activities that finance professionals perform to fulfil these roles. Consequently, it is the foundation of the whole qualification and answers the question: what do finance professionals do and why? It provides links with other topics within the subject and what is covered in other areas of the Operational Level.

Lead outcome	Component outcome	Topics to be covered	Explanatory notes
1. Explain the roles of the finance function in organisations.	Explain how the finance function: a. Enables organisations to create and preserve value b. Shapes how organisations create and preserve value c. Narrates how organisations create and preserve value	• The fast-changing and unpredictable contexts in which organisations operate • Enabling value creation through planning, forecasting and resource allocation • Shaping value creation through performance management and control • Narrating the value creation story through corporate reporting • The role of ethics in the role of the finance function	Describe the increasingly disruptive contexts in which organisations and their finance teams operate and how these contexts shape the role of finance. Take each role and show how finance performs it in a typical organisational setting. The coverage should be introductory and brief. It is meant to set the scene for subsequent sections and draw a link between the roles and the topics that will be covered in other areas of the Operational Level.
2. Describe the activities that finance professionals perform to fulfil the roles.	Describe how the finance function: a. Collates data to prepare information about organisations b. Provides insight to users by analysing information c. Communicates insight to influence users d. Supports the implementation of decisions to achieve the desired impact e. Connects the different activities connect to each other	• How data is collected, cleaned and connected by finance • Types of analysis to produce insights • How finance communicates to influence key stakeholders (audiences, frequency, format, etc.) • How finance uses resource allocation and performance management to enable organisations to achieve their objectives • Potential impact of technology	Use 'information to impact' framework to describe the primary activities finance professionals perform. Relate it to how data is generated, transformed and used. Link it to how technology could be used to improve the productivity of finance professionals in these areas and the threat of automation.

E1B: Technology in a Digital World

This section focuses on the technologies that define and drive the digital world in which finance operates. It provides awareness of the technologies used in organisations and deepens understanding of the impact of the technologies on what finance does. It draws on the issues raised in the previous section about the role of finance and the activities finance performs to fulfil these roles. Given that the digital world is underpinned by technology and the use of data, this section provides a foundation to the next section on data.

Lead outcome	Component outcome	Topics to be covered	Explanatory notes
1. Outline and explain the technologies that affect business and finance.	a. Outline the key features of the fourth industrial revolution. b. Outline and explain the key technologies that define and drive the digital world.	• Characteristics and dynamics of the fourth industrial revolution • Cloud computing • Big data analytics • Process automation • Artificial intelligence • Data visualisation • Blockchain • Internet of things • Mobile • 3-D printing	The aim is to create awareness of the technologies that drive the digital world and how they interact with each other. The technologies outlined by the major advisory firms and the World Economic Forum digital transformation initiative provide the material on which learning and related activities can be based.
2. Examine how the finance function uses digital technologies to fulfil its roles.	Examine how finance uses the following to guide how it performs its roles: a. Digital technology b. Digital mindsets c. Automation and the future of work d. Ethics of technology usage	• How finance uses technologies listed above • Areas of finance susceptible to automation and why • New areas for finance to focus on • Digital mindsets for finance • Ethics of the use of technology	Examine how finance professionals use the relevant technologies to fulfil their roles. Explain how the technologies affect various activities finance professionals perform in the 'information to impact' framework. The intention is to move from creating awareness to generating understanding of how finance can use these technologies to increase its value and relevance to organisations.

E1C: Data and Information in a Digital World

This section draws out one of the major implications of using technology in organisations and the finance function – namely the collection and processing of information can be done more effectively by machines rather than by people. It asserts that the role of finance professionals should be to use data to create and preserve value for organisations. Five ways of using data are examined. The key competencies required to use data in these ways are also highlighted. The primary objective is to help finance professionals understand what they can do with data and how to build the skills needed to use data.

Lead outcome	Component outcome	Topics to be covered	Explanatory notes
1. Describe the ways in which data is used by the finance function.	Identify the ways in which the finance function uses data: a. In a general sense b. Specifically in each of the primary activities of finance	Using data for: • Decision-making • Understanding the customer • Developing customer value proposition • Enhancing operational efficiency • Monetising data • Ethics of data usage	Build on the previous section on technology to explain why, in the digital world, finance professionals must place more focus on using information than on collecting and/or processing information. Outline and describe the various uses of information. Link them to the primary activities that the finance function performs and to the topics to be covered in other modules of the Operational Level.
2. Explain the competencies required to use data to create and preserve value for organisations.	Explain the competencies that finance professionals need in: a. Data strategy and planning b. Data engineering, extraction and mining c. Data modelling, manipulation and analysis d. Data and insight communication	• Assessment of data needs • Extraction, transformation and loading (ETL) systems • Business Intelligence (BI) systems • Big data analytics • Data visualisation	Highlight and explain the data competencies required in the digital world. Locate where finance has a competitive advantage and where finance will need to work with data scientists.

E1D: Shape and Structure of the Finance function

This section brings together the implications of the previous sections. It reveals how the finance function is structured and shaped. This structure and shape enables finance to perform its role in the organisation and with other internal and external stakeholders. In this sense, it prepares candidates for the next section, which looks at how finance interacts with key internal stakeholders in operations, marketing and human resources.

Lead outcome	Component outcome	Topics to be covered	Explanatory notes
1. Describe the structure and shape of the finance function.	Describe the: a. Evolution of the shape of the finance function b. Shape of the finance function in the digital era	• Structure of the finance function from the roles that generate information to the roles that turn information into insight and communicate insight to decision-makers • Hierarchical shape of finance function • Shared services and outsourcing of finance operations • Retained finance • Automation and diamond shape of finance function	Introduce candidates to the structure of the finance function and outline the broad areas of finance such as finance operations, external reporting, financial planning and analysis (FP&A), decision support etc. Describe the evolving shape of the finance function from the triangle to the diamond shape. Link the description to the impact of digital technology and automation on the finance function.
2. Explain what each level of the finance function does.	Explain the activities of: a. Finance operations b. Specialist areas including financial reporting and financial planning and analysis (FP&A) c. Strategic partnering for value d. Strategic leadership of the finance team	• Finance operations to generate information and preliminary insight • FP&A, taxation, corporate reporting, decision support to produce insight • Business partnering to influence organisation to make appropriate decisions • Leading the finance team to create the required impact for the organisation	The focus is the diamond shape and the four levels within this shape. Explain what each level does, the relationship between the levels, and the link between the levels and the basic finance activities covered under the role of finance.

E1E: Finance Interacting with the Organisation

The finance function is not the only area of activity in organisations. Finance joins with others to create and preserve value for their organisations. This section brings together what has been learned in the previous section to describe how finance can interact with other parts of the organisation to achieve the objectives of finance, those other areas and crucially the objectives of the whole organisation. The aim is to show how finance can work collaboratively in a connected (and joined-up) organisation and not in isolation.

Lead outcome	Component outcome	Topics to be covered	Explanatory notes
1. Describe how the finance function interacts with operations.	Describe: a. Main role of operations b. Areas of interface with finance c. Key performance indicators	• Process management • Product and service management • Supply chain management	Describe how finance plays its role by interacting with the rest of the organisation. Bring together the issues raised in the previous sections and link them to what the other areas of the organisations do. For example, address how finance and marketing interact using data and collaborative technology to achieve organisational goals and the individual functional goals of both finance and marketing. Describe how the use of KPIs influence these interactions and how the KPIs of finance and these areas can be aligned to ensure they work together effectively.
2. Describe how the finance function interacts with sales and marketing.	Describe: a. Main role of sales and marketing b. Areas of interface with finance c. Key performance indicators	• Market segmentation • Big data analytics in marketing • Channel management • Sales forecasting and management	
3. Describe how the finance function interacts with human resources.	Describe: a. Main role of human resources b. Areas of interface with finance c. Key performance indicators	• Staff acquisition • Staff development • Performance management • Motivation and reward systems	
4. Describe how the finance function interacts with IT.	Describe: a. Main role of IT b. Areas of interface with finance c. Key performance indicators	• IT infrastructure • IT systems support • Costs and benefits of IT systems	

Section 1

OBJECTIVE TEST QUESTIONS

All the section objective questions carry the same number of marks.

SYLLABUS SECTION A: ROLE OF THE FINANCE FUNCTION

1   Stan is trying to work out how many staff members are going to be required to work on a project next week.

Which role of the finance function best describes what Stan is doing?

A   Resource allocation

B   Performance management and control

C   Planning

D   Financial (corporate) reporting

2   Performance measures can be both qualitative and quantitative.

Which of the following would be classified as quantitative performance measures?

Select three that apply.

A   Customer satisfaction rating

B   Sales

C   Level of innovation

D   Staff productivity

E   Profit

F   Units produced

3   **Match the following descriptions to the ethical principle they describe.**

Completing work carefully, thoroughly and diligently, in accordance with relevant technical and professional standards.	Integrity
Being straightforward, honest and truthful in all professional and business relationships.	Confidentiality
Non-disclosure of information unless you have specific permission or a legal or professional duty to do so.	Professional behaviour
Not allowing bias, conflict of interest, or the influence of other people to override your professional judgement.	Professional competence and due care
Compliance with relevant laws and regulations.	Objectivity

4   Polly, a CIMA member in practice, has been asked to complete an important task. However, she is very pushed for time and knows she will not be able to complete it properly.

Which ethical principle is under threat?

A   Integrity

B   Confidentiality

C   Professional competence and due care

D   Professional behaviour

E   Objectivity

5   Gemma, a CIMA member in practice, has been told by her boss that there are going to be some redundancies in the company. She has been reassured that her job is safe but has been told of a number of colleagues whose jobs are at risk. One of these colleagues is a close friend of Gemma who she knows is about to buy a new house.

If Gemma warns her friend about the redundancy plans which ethical principle is under threat?

A   Integrity

B   Confidentiality

C   Professional competence and due care

D   Professional behaviour

E   Objectivity

6 **Which three of the following are BENEFITS of a company behaving in an ethical manner?**

A   Improve reputation

B   Attract high calibre employees

C   Increased costs

D   Increased risk

E   Increased sales

7 **Which of the following would be considered to be connected stakeholders?**

Select three that apply.

A   Employees

B   Government

C   Environmental pressure groups

D   Suppliers

E   Customer

F   Lenders

8 The directors of ECC Ltd are proposing the introduction of many CSR initiatives. However, their shareholders are not convinced that it is worth the increased cost to the business.

Which of the following are arguments FOR the introduction of CSR initiatives?

Select three that apply

A   Strengthens the brand

B   Acts as a method of differentiation

C   Increases costs

D   Attracts new customers

E   Is a public relations (PR) exercise

9 The risk that the directors may run the company in their own interests, rather than those of the shareholders is known as the agency problem.

True or false?

10 **Which of the following symptoms can indicate that there is poor corporate governance?**

Select three that apply.

A   Increasing contact with shareholders

B   Domination of the board

C   Lack of internal audit

D   Emphasis on long term profitability

E   Lack of supervision of employees

11 **Which of the following statements is/are true?**

(i) In the UK, Corporate Governance is a principles based system.

(ii) In the US, Corporate Governance is a rules based system.

A Statement (i) only

B Statement (ii) only

C Neither of them

D Both of them

12 The finance function has three main roles; it 'enables', 'shapes how' and 'narrates how' value is created and preserved.

Which of the following would the finance function carry out to 'shape how' the organisation creates and preserves value?

A Performance management and control

B Planning and forecasting

C Financial (corporate) reporting

D Planning, forecasting and resource allocation

13 **Using the principles of good corporate governance, which committees should a company make use of?**

Select three that apply.

A Nominations committee

B Remuneration committee

C Ethics committee

D Governance committee

E Board committee

F Audit committee

14 **According to the UK Corporate Governance Code, a company can improve corporate governance by ensuring that:**

A The chairman and chief executive are the same individual in order to avoid confusion over who has responsibility for running the company.

B The chairman and chief executive are different individuals in case one dies or becomes ill.

C The company chairman is remunerated in line with the performance of the company.

D The chairman and chief executive are different individuals in order to prevent one person having too much power within the company.

15 Kay is a senior employee of Henshaw plc and is considering becoming a NED after she retires.

   After how many years will she be classified as an independent NED?

   A   4 years

   B   5 years

   C   6 years

   D   7 years

16 Churchman plc is looking to appoint new members to its board of directors, which committee should they consult before making such appointments?

   A   Appointments committee

   B   Directors committee

   C   Committee of NEDs

   D   Nominations committee

17 The argument that companies should operate solely to make money for shareholders and that it is not a company's role to worry about social responsibilities is the viewpoint of:

   A   Modernists

   B   Everyone

   C   Traditionalists

   D   The government

18 What are the three classifications of stakeholders commonly known as?

   A   Internal, external, connected

   B   Shareholders, employees, customers

   C   Internal, external, regulated

   D   Connected, unconnected, external

19 Match the stakeholder with their need/expectation of the company

Stakeholder	Need/expectation
Government	Pay, working conditions and job security
Shareholders	Dividends and capital growth
Employees	Provision of taxes and jobs and compliance with legislation
Customers	Value-for-money products and services

20   Which of the following statements is/are true?

(i)   The chairman is the person in charge of running the company.

(ii)   The chief economic officer is the person in charge of running the company.

A   Statement (i)

B   Statement (ii)

C   Both of them

D   Neither of them

21   Complete the following sentences by placing one of the following options in the spaces.

The preparation of forecasts, for example of future sales or material prices, will be an important role of the finance function _____ .

The preparation of comprehensive reports for shareholders will be an important role of the finance function _____.

The preparation of variance analysis for control purposes will be an important role of the finance function _____.

Options:
in narrating how the organisation creates and preserves value
in enabling the organisation to create and preserve value
in shaping how the organisation creates and preserves value

22   Which of the following organisations is normally found in the public sector?

A   Schools

B   Charities

C   Clubs

D   Businesses

23   Which of the following statements is/are true?

(i)   The main IFRS (International Financial Reporting Standards) rarely change that much and so it can be broadly assumed that these basics will remain fixed in the medium term.

(ii)   The finance function merely records what has happened over the period in question and as long as it can do that it shouldn't need to be proactive in the way that it is organised.

A   Statement (i)

B   Statement (ii)

C   Both of them

D   Neither of them

24   **Which of the following is an example of poor corporate social responsibility?**

    A   The sacking of an employee for gross misconduct

    B   Building a product with a known failure rate

    C   The advertising of cigarettes on early evening TV

    D   A significant redundancy programme

25   **What is the generally accepted definition of agency risk?**

    A   The risk that agency staff are less experienced than fulltime employees and hence are more likely to make mistakes.

    B   The risk that government agencies will interfere with the company's procedures resulting in excessive costs.

    C   Directors, as agents of the owners will act in a way that is contrary to the wishes of those owners.

    D   Employees, as agents to the directors will act in a way that is contrary to the wishes of those directors.

26   Changes brought about by technology are greatly changing the shape of the finance function. However, not-for-profit organisations will not be affected as their primary objective is not a profit motive.

    Is this statement true or false?

27   **Which of the following TWO statements are true with regards to change in the modern world?**

    A   Change always increases the risks faced by an organisation

    B   Change is so unpredictable that there is no point in having long term plans

    C   A key driver of change in the modern world is the rapid advancements in technology

    D   Changing customers' expectations cannot be ignored if a business wants to remain competitive

    E   Change does not affect really small enterprises

28   Jemima has been asked to collect some information for her manager. It takes her 14 hours to gather the information and when she presents it to her manager it is immediately filed away.

    Which of the characteristics of good quality information is not being exhibited?

    A   Understandable

    B   Complete

    C   Cost < benefit

    D   Accurate

29 **Which of the following is NOT one of the 5 As of a finance professional's basic activities?**

A Assemble

B Apply

C Acumen

D Advise

E Align

30 **Which of the 5 As of a finance professional's basic activities includes collecting data from a variety of sources?**

A Acumen

B Advise

C Assemble

D Adapt

E Accumulate

31 **True or false, data consists of raw fact and figures whilst information is data that has been processed?**

32 **Which of the 5 As of a finance professional's basic activities includes comparing actual information to budgeted information?**

A Assemble

B Analyse

C Advise

D Apply

E Acumen

33 **Which three of the following may be limitations of using external data sources?**

A It may be out of date

B It may be more difficult to gather

C It has no relevance to the organisation using it

D It may not be accurate

E It is unethical to use someone else's data

34 **Which type of information cannot normally be expressed in numerical terms?**

A   Quantitative

B   Qualitative

C   Financial

D   Non-financial

35 **Which three of the following are examples of internal sources of data?**

A   Purchase ledger data

B   Payroll data

C   Newspaper articles

D   Exchange rate data

E   Production data

36 **At what stage within the information to impact framework is the finance function most predominantly focussed on guidance and management?**

A   Information

B   Insight

C   Influence

D   Impact

37 David is examining a report that has been prepared by a junior member of the finance team. He has noticed there are a lot of spelling mistakes and not all of the figures add up.

Which of the characteristics of "good" information is not being exhibited?

A   Accurate

B   Complete

C   Understandable

D   Relevant

38 Eliza is currently in the process of comparing budgeted sales data to actual data and trying to investigate reasons for the variances.

Using the information to impact framework, which stage would best describe Eliza's current activity?

A   Information

B   Insight

C   Influence

D   Impact

39 Which of the following statements regarding the analysis of quantitative data is correct?

A   Sales growth of 20% year on year represents significant growth.

B   Non-financial data cannot be quantified and therefore has less analysis value than financial data.

C   Good quality analysis relies upon a representative sample of the population.

D   Number of training days taken per employee is not an example of quantitative data.

40 During which stage of the information to impact framework are solutions typically deployed?

A   Information

B   Insight

C   Influence

D   Impact

SYLLABUS SECTION B: TECHNOLOGY IN A DIGITAL WORLD

41 "A rapid and major change in an economy, driven by a shift in the methods and types of work undertaken" best describes what?

A   Globalisation

B   An industrial revolution

C   The digital age

D   Political instability

42 How is the delivery of on-demand computing resources otherwise known?

A   Artificial Intelligence

B   The Internet of Things

C   Big Data

D   Cloud computing

43 The process by which users log on to remote servers to access and process their files is best known as what?

A   Cloud computing

B   Wide Area Network

C   The internet

D   Remote working

44   **What are the two main types of cloud computing?**

A   Public Cloud

B   Restricted Cloud

C   Private Cloud

D   Amazon Cloud

45   **Which three of the following are disadvantages of cloud computing?**

A   Scalability

B   Contract management

C   Potential job losses

D   Reliance on a third party

E   Increases cost

F   Reduced flexibility for employees

46   **Which of the following statements relating to big data are true?**

Select three that apply.

A   Big data refers to any financial data over $1 billion

B   The defining characteristics of big data are velocity, volume and variety

C   Managing big data effectively can lead to increased competitive advantage

D   The term big data means 'data that comes from many sources'

E   Big data contains both financial and non-financial data

47   **How might the following sources of data be classified?**

Select from the following: Human Sourced, Machine Generated, Processed, Open

A   National Statistics

B   Social media posts

C   Emails

D   Smart meters

E   Customer database

F   Census

G   Home assistants

H   Fixed asset register

48 **Which one of the following sentences is true?**

A   Process automation is only feasible for simple, repetitive tasks

B   Process automation in complex business areas is beyond the limits of technology

C   Process automation can enable a business to save costs

D   Process automation usually leads to employee dissatisfaction

49 **Machines working and reacting like human beings describes what?**

A   Robotics

B   Voice recognition

C   Artificial intelligence

D   The 4th Industrial Revolution

50 **Which one of the following is a definition of a blockchain?**

A   A technology that allows people who do not know each other to trust a shared record of events.

B   A centralised, undistributed and private digital ledger that is used to record transactions.

C   A sequence of transactions facilitated by the internet.

D   A supply chain management system used to improve efficiency.

51 **Which three of the following statements about a blockchain are true?**

A   Blockchain is regarded as a solution to cyber security risk

B   Records in the blockchain are publically available

C   Records in the blockchain are kept private to enhance security

D   The verification of transactions is carried out by computers

E   The verification of transaction is carried out by individuals

52 **What is the Internet of Things?**

A   An interactive collection of websites enabling users to communicate with one another.

B   A technology that allows people who do not know each other to trust a shared record of events.

C   Smart phones that enable users to control appliances within their home such as their heating or lighting.

D   A network of smart devices with inbuilt software and connectivity which connect to the internet.

53 **True or false, advancements in mobile technology have contributed to the decline in the newspaper industry?**

54 CDMA is the technology that has transformed mobile technology.

What does CDMA stand for?

A   Coded data mobile application

B   Code-division multiple access

C   Cloud data mobile access

D   Computer device mobile acceleration

55 **How is "additive manufacturing", creating a product layer by layer, better known?**

A   Cellular manufacturing

B   Lean manufacturing

C   3-D printing

D   Blockchain technology

56 **Which three of the following are consequences of the developments in mobile technologies?**

A   The decline of the newspaper industry

B   The decline of social media interactions

C   The decline in the banking industry

D   An increase in the on demand nature of music

E   An increase in the cost to manufacture smart devices

57 **Which three of the following are advantages of 3-D printing?**

A   Gaining economies of scale through the ability to batch produce

B   Increased throughput speed from design to print

C   Off-cuts can be recycled into future products

D   Maintenance of Intellectual Property

E   Customisation of design leading to competitive advantage

58 **Which three of the following are advantages of cloud computing?**

A   Cost efficiency

B   Scalability

C   Flexibility

D   Contract management

E   Career opportunities

F   Highlights inefficiencies

59 Assessing the reliability of big data refers to which of the 4 Vs?

A   Velocity

B   Volume

C   Visibility

D   Veracity

60 Which of the following statements about data visualisation is true?

A   The most common use of data visualisation is the creation of a dashboard displaying real time KPIs.

B   Data is always displayed in standardised formats to ensure consistency.

C   Data visualisation refers to data that is analysed using virtual reality software.

D   Increased use of data visualisation within organisations increases the need for more IT experts.

61 Technologies which are anticipated to update existing systems to improve capability are often referred to as what?

A   Core modernisation tools

B   Exponentials

C   Innovators

D   The digital age

62 Technologies which will deliver new capabilities are often referred to as what?

A   Core modernisation tools

B   Exponentials

C   Innovators

D   The digital age

63 Which of the following is a disadvantage of cloud computing?

A   Increased flexibility to working arrangements

B   Less reliance on third party suppliers

C   Access to continually up to date software

D   Easier integration of systems

64 True or false, cloud computing enables multiple users to collaborate on a file at the same time, although this increases the risk of version control issues.

A   True

B   False

65 **Which three of the following are advantages of investing in process automation?**

A   Staff time can be freed up to focus on value adding activities

B   No extra training will be required for staff as they will no longer be processing manually

C   Staff will automatically buy in to having the mundane work taken from them

D   Headcount reductions

E   Improved efficiency

66 **The provision of information in a more appealing and understandable manner is often referred to as what?**

A   Artificial Intelligence

B   Data simplification

C   Cloud computing

D   Data visualisation

67 **Which of the following is not necessarily a benefit of data visualisation?**

A   Improves the accuracy of the data being analysed

B   Problem areas can be identified sooner

C   Understandable by many users

D   Improved decision making

68 **Which of the following statements regarding blockchain are true?**

(i)   Blockchain technology involves the use of a distributed ledger.

(ii)   Digital assets such as cryptocurrencies should be considered as intangible assets in the financial statements.

(iii) The use of blockchain technologies removes the need for traditional intermediaries in transactions.

(iv)   Blockchain solutions will not overcome the issue of slow cross border payments.

A   (i) and (ii)

B   (i) and (iii)

C   (iii) and (iv)

D   (i), (ii) and (iii)

69 **How has 3-D printing primarily impacted the finance function?**

A   Impacted the costings of operations

B   Facilitated the creation of assets

C   Driven higher revenues

D   Increased inventories

70 Which of the following are qualities identified by Forbes as being important dimensions of the digital mind set?

Select three that apply.

A   Provide vision yet empower others

B   Have the imagination to innovate

C   Be sceptical yet open minded

D   Sustain yet disrupt

E   Retain control yet open minded

71 Book-my-room is a broker facilitating the letting of private accommodation between individuals.

Which one of the following is a likely consequence for their financial statements?

A   Their network of contracts will be recognised as an intangible asset on their statement of financial position.

B   The true value of Book-my-room may be understated on their statement of financial position.

C   The expenses on the statement of profit or loss will be overstated.

D   Their statement of cashflows will be reduced as the private individuals sort payment of the lettings out between themselves.

72 Which one of the following statements about big data and the internal audit function are true?

A   The emergence of big data has improved the accuracy of data which means smaller sample sizes now need to be tested.

B   Internal audit will now be testing and analysing larger populations of data.

C   Big data has no relevance to the internal audit function.

D   Big data will contribute to the development of more efficient and insightful management control systems and budgeting processes.

73 True or false, cryptocurrencies should be accounted for as cash and cash equivalents on the statement of financial position?

A   True

B   False

74 So Handy is a relatively young business comprising a franchised network of labourers such as plumbers, electricians and carpenters. Each franchisee has an app that enables them to log and record the expenses they incur as well as scanning all receipts for materials purchased.

What type of technology are they making use of?

A   Social media

B   Internet of things

C   An intranet

D   Mobile technology

75 Technological developments are driving an increase in process automation. Consequently, some of the traditional skills of a finance professional such as data collection and processing will need to be replaced with higher-level skills.

Which skill is required to make decisions and evaluate data sources?

A   Analytical skills

B   People skills

C   Judgement

D   Leadership

76 During her appraisal interview, Edie's line manager praises her for having a good understanding of the business environment.

Which essential skill is Edie displaying?

A   Business acumen

B   Leadership skills

C   Judgement

D   Analytical skills

77 **Which three of the following are principles within GDPR?**

A   Data must not be kept for longer than five years

B   Data must be used for a specified, explicit purpose

C   Data held must be accurate

D   Data must be used transparently

78 **True or false, compliance with GDPR is the only thing that matters where data usage is concerned?**

A   True

B   False

79 Corporate digital responsibility (CDR) involves a commitment to protect customers.

Which two of the following statements are true about CDR?

    A   It demonstrates an awareness of the risks associated with data

    B   It is unnecessary as all data regulations are covered within GDPR

    C   It is a voluntary commitment to go beyond mere compliance with legislation

    D   It is a legal requirement for any organisation that holds data about its customers

80 In the context of CDR, which of the following is an example of "digital inclusion"

    A   Incentivising customers to give more data

    B   The customer's ability to opt in and be rewarded for sharing data

    C   A pharmaceutical company donating clinical trial data to a university

    D   A bank using a customer's financial information to help them improve their financial management

SYLLABUS SECTION C: DATA AND INFORMATION IN A DIGITAL WORLD

81 Match each of the below individuals to the level of decision making they are involved in.

Pick from the following options: Strategic, Tactical and Operational

Jane is reviewing the staffing rota for the coming week to see if extra staff are needed.

Bill is a director of the company currently involved in an acquisition decision.

Colleen is choosing which products will be stocked in each of the stores around the country.

82 True or false? Providing insightful information to the organisation can enhance the competitive advantage, however, will also always increase the costs to the business.

    A   True

    B   False

83 Which three of the following are ways that data and technology can support the marketing function?

    A   Comparing prices with competitors

    B   Assessing the viability of market segments

    C   Improving efficiencies in the supply chain

    D   Preventative maintenance of products

    E   Personalising communications with customers

84   **Which three of the following are ways that data and technology can support operations?**

    A   Identifying bottlenecks in processes

    B   Preventative maintenance of products

    C   Forecasting production

    D   Identifying training needs of employees

    E   Targeting customers with offers

85   **Images, audio files and animations are all examples of what?**

    A   Technology

    B   Big data

    C   Information

    D   Digital assets

86   Taylor Training Co produced a bank of educational videos that students can access at any time to support their learning.

    These videos are examples of what for Taylor Training Co?

    A   Tangible non-current asset

    B   Digital asset

    C   Video asset

    D   Customer asset

87   **Which two of the following are features of a DAMS?**

    A   Decentralised digital asset access

    B   Open access to any user

    C   Facilitated by cloud based software

    D   Single central location for digital asset storage

88   **True or False? Because digital assets are stored on the cloud it makes them less secure than if they were stored on a hard drive**

    A   True

    B   False

89   **How are medium term decisions better known?**

    A   Strategic

    B   Managerial

    C   Operational

    D   Tactical

90   What does the acronym DAMS stand for?

   A   Data and marketing strategy

   B   Digitised automatic management system

   C   Digital asset management system

   D   Data assisted management strategy

91   There are three levels of decision making; strategic, tactical and operational.

   In this context which of the following statement is/are true?

   (i)   Strategic decisions are clearly important but without good tactical support, good strategic decisions may never be realised.

   (ii)   Operational decision making may be last of the three but poor operational decisions will often cause costs to spiral out of control.

   A   (i) only

   B   (ii) only

   C   Both are true

   D   Neither are true

92   Which of the following would be correctly described as information to the sales director of a business?

   A   The invoice total of a sale made

   B   The average daily sales per department

   C   The lead time expected on raw materials

   D   The sales price list for the company products

93   How many connected devices are there expected to be on the planet by 2020?

   A   5 billion

   B   50 billion

   C   100 billion

   D   200 billion

94   In the context of data gathering and quality, which of the following statements are true?

   (i)   The technology available merely takes the legwork out of data gathering, everything that is available now was available in the past, but it was too time consuming to gather it.

   (ii)   With the improved data comes with it the need to be able to respond quickly. Shorter lead times are an essential aspect of improved data.

   A   (i) only

   B   (ii) only

   C   Both are true

   D   Neither are true

95 In the context of digital asset management systems (DAMS) which of the following statements are true?

(i) Once someone has permission to use (say) an image there is nothing to stop them sharing that image with others.

(ii) Once someone has permission to use (say) an image then there is nothing to stop them using that image for longer than it was intended.

A (i) only

B (ii) only

C Both are true

D Neither are true

96 Which of the following best describes tactical decision making?

A Long-term decisions made by senior management

B Decisions made repeatedly over the short term

C Decisions which impact the entire organisation

D Decisions involving putting the strategic plan into action

97 Beth and her colleagues at the same level of the organisational hierarchy are in discussions about which, if any, acquisitions to make using the surplus funds of the business. They are choosing between two similar businesses.

Which level of decision making are they engaging in?

A Strategic

B Tactical

C Acquisitional

D Operational

98 Maypole ltd has been analysing various aspects of the data that it collects. Their data analyst has identified that parents with children of a particular age are regularly searching for products on their website.

Which benefit of data analytics is specifically being exhibited?

A Enhanced data transparency

B Efficiency gains

C Enhanced performance

D Market customisation

99 Data which gives insight into the relationship between a product launch and subsequent sales helps with which one aspect of the marketing mix?

A Product

B Price

C Place

D Promotion

100 Connecting machines on the internet of things to collect real time data has many advantages for a manufacturing business.

Monitoring the performance of the machines enables which of the following advantages specifically?

A Forecasting

B Preventative maintenance

C Improved service for customers

D Supply chain collaboration

101 Which stakeholder of the finance function is most likely to require data on competitors' pricing strategies?

A Sales

B Production

C Shareholders

D Employees

102 Which stakeholder of the finance function is most likely to require data on employee productivity?

A Production

B Employees

C HR

D Shareholders

103 Which stakeholder of the finance function is most likely to require data on carbon footprint?

A Employees

B Sales

C Production

D Shareholders

104 **Which stakeholder of the finance function is most likely to require data visualisations on key metrics?**

    A   Directors

    B   Shareholders

    C   HR

    D   Sales

105 **What are the three stages in transferring data? (in the correct order)**

    A   Loading, extraction, transformation

    B   Input, process, output

    C   Extraction, transformation, loading

    D   Extraction, converting, warehousing

106 A data model considers the data of an organisation in a systematic way that allows it to be stored and retrieved in an efficient and effective manner.

Match the level of data modelling with its description

Level	Description
Conceptual	This level begins to develop a technical map of rules and data structures defining how data will be held and used
Logical	This considers how the defined system requirements will be implemented using a specific database management system
Physical	Business oriented and practical, considering the business data and its requirements

107 **What can be described as "a coherent approach for organising, governing, analysing and deploying an organisations information assets"**

    A   Digital assets

    B   Data strategy

    C   Business Intelligence

    D   Data warehousing

108 **What does "the process of changing data to make it easier to read" describe?**

    A   Data mining

    B   Data manipulation

    C   Data modelling

    D   Data query

109 **Which of the 4 Vs of big data refers to the constant stream of data being produced?**

    A   Variety

    B   Veracity

    C   Volume

    D   Velocity

110 **What does "the technology driven process of analysing business data" describe?**

    A   Business intelligence

    B   Big data

    C   Data strategy

    D   Data visualisation

111 **Which of the following best describes an ETL system?**

    A   The process of harvesting data from source locations

    B   The transformation of data into a suitable format

    C   The uploading of clan data into a data warehouse

    D   A single tool to automatically bring data sources into a destination system

112 **The use of a dashboard to present data is an example of what?**

    A   Data visualisation

    B   Data simplification

    C   Graphical data

    D   Information processing

113 **The need for systems to validate data links to which of the 4 Vs of big data?**

    A   Variety

    B   Veracity

    C   Volume

    D   Velocity

114 **Which stakeholder is likely to be most interested in data about the productivity of individual staff members?**

    A   External auditors

    B   Customers

    C   Internal auditors

    D   Shareholders

115 Interest cover, market value of non-current assets and the amount of existing loans are all types of data of most interest to:

A   Shareholders

B   Directors

C   Employees

D   Lenders

116 In relation to data, which of the following statements are true?

(i)   One cannot have too much data, so an organisation should gather as much as possible.

(ii) As far as sales prices are concerned a sales director just needs the average sales price achieved in the most recent reporting period to manage the business.

A   (i) only

B   (ii) only

C   Both are true

D   Neither are true

117 An effective data strategy should consist of five elements; identify, store, provision, process and which other?

A   Responsibility

B   Manage

C   Govern

D   Congruence

118 Which of the following is not a level in a data modelling process?

A   Physical

B   Structural

C   Conceptual

D   Logical

119 In the context of an ETL system, which of the following statements are true?

(i)   Data is extracted and then profiled before being loaded in to the data warehouse.

(ii) Once data is profiled it is transformed to a suitable form before being extracted and loaded in to the data warehouse.

A   (i) only

B   (ii) only

C   Both are true

D   Neither are true

120 ELC Co has produced some infographics to enable the visualisation of its sales data. Which three of the following characteristics will make the infographics more effective?

A Details of sales made to each customer on a daily basis

B The ability to drill down to obtain further detail

C Avoidance of technical jargon

D Access granted to all sales staff

E Intuitive visualisations needing little explanation

SYLLABUS SECTION D: SHAPE AND STRUCTURE OF THE FINANCE FUNCTION

121 Which of the following statements regarding the entrepreneurial structure is correct?

A It usually allows for defined career paths for employees

B It often enjoys strong goal congruence throughout the organisation

C It can normally cope with significant diversification and growth

D Control within the organisation tends to be weak

122 Which of the following is a disadvantage of a functional structure?

A Lack of economies of scale

B Absence of standardisation

C Specialists feel isolated

D Empire building

123 Which of the following is a characteristic of a matrix structure?

A Built around the owner manager, who makes all the decisions.

B Appropriate for small companies which have few products and locations and which exist in a relatively stable environment.

C Structured in accordance with product lines or divisions or departments.

D Requires dual reporting to managers, for example when a project team member has to report to a project manager as well as a head of his functional department.

124 The following are attributes of either divisional or functional structures.

Which two of the following are features of the divisional structure?

A Economies of scale are encouraged

B Encourages standardisation of outputs and processes

C Adaptable if further diversification is pursued

D Senior managers are able to focus on strategic issues

125 H Co makes a variety of unrelated products, including bicycles, furniture and electronics. It is aware that each of these products requires very different strategies and functions. H wishes to use a structure that will allow for each product to be managed separately, but wishes to minimise its overall administrative costs.

Which of the following organisational structures would be most appropriate for H Co to adopt?

A   Divisional

B   Entrepreneurial

C   Functional

D   Matrix

126 **Which of the following structures results in a potential loss of control over key operating decisions and a reduction in goal congruence?**

A   Matrix

B   Entrepreneurial

C   Functional

D   Geographic

127 **In relation to organisational structures which of the following is the correct definition of the phrase 'span of control'?**

A   The number of employees that a manager is directly responsible for

B   The number of management levels in an organisational structure

C   The number of levels in the hierarchy below a given manager

D   The number of managers in the organisation

128 **Correctly label the diagram using the options below**

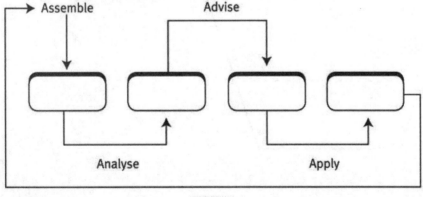

A   Impact

B   Insight

C   Influence

D   Information

129 Which of the finance functions basic activities have more the greatest emphasis on accounting and governance rather than guidance and management?

A   Assemble

B   Analyse

C   Advise

D   Apply

130 Complete the following sentence to explain the development of the contemporary finance function.

Pick from the following words: innovation, assembly, advising, technology, analysis, automation, applying/execution

_____ and_____ will play an important role in all of the activities of the finance function but will have the largest impact on the _____ and_____ activities.

This will 'free up' the resource of the finance function professionals who can now place greater focus on the_____ and _____activities.

131 The shape of the finance function is changing into a diamond shape with four levels. Label the following diagram to show each of the levels.

Pick from the following: digital centres of excellence, smart finance factories, strategic business partnering, senior finance team

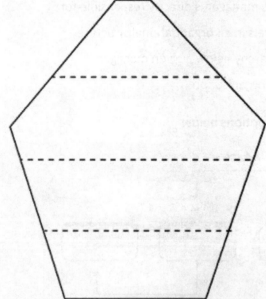

132 Which of the following statements about outsourcing is/are correct?

Statement	True?
An advantage of outsourcing is reduced headcount and therefore reduced cost.	
Outsourcing can enable an organisation to access expertise that it might otherwise be lacking.	
A drawback of outsourcing is that it distracts management and they lose focus of their core activities.	
Transaction costs are a benefit to the business.	
Outsourcing may lead to redundancies which can affect employee morale.	

133 Which of the following are advantages of setting up a shared service centre for the finance function?

Select three that apply

A   Systems consolidation

B   Increased control

C   Empire building

D   Consistency of reporting

E   Advancements in technology

F   It makes it easier to deal with cultural or language differences

134 Transaction costs are expenses resulting from which one of the following?

A   Outsourcing of services

B   Off-shoring of organisational functions

C   Penetration pricing

D   Organisational downsizing

135 Complete the sentence below by placing one of the following options in the space.

One of the main activities of the finance function is 'advising to influence'. Broadly speaking this can be referred to as _____.

| REPORTING | DEPLOYING SOLUTIONS | QUESTIONING | DEVELOPING SOLUTIONS |

136 Complete the sentence below by placing one of the following options in the space.

A radical transformation and fundamental rethinking of business processes is called:

| BPR | KAIZEN | TQM | RPA |

137 **Which level of the finance function is more likely to focus on information for external stakeholders?**

    A   Operational

    B   Management

    C   Strategic

    D   External

138 Harry works in a large organisation which has both suppliers and customers all over the world. Harry is a CIMA qualified accountant and is responsible for managing foreign currency. In particular, Harry tries to minimise the company's exposure to foreign exchange losses.

    What is Harry's role?

    A   Treasurer

    B   Management accountant

    C   Financial accountant

    D   Internal audit

139 **With regards to the management accounting function, which one of the following statements is correct?**

    A   It is often used by external stakeholders, such as shareholders

    B   It is a requirement for all limited companies

    C   It is mainly a historic record of the organisation's activities

    D   It aids planning and decision making within the business

140 **K Co has recently split its accounting function into two parts – one that deals with management accounting and the other with financial accounting.**

    A   Management accounting

    B   Financial accounting

    Match the following statements to either A (management accounting) or B (financial accounting).

    (i)   Preparation of the statement of profit or loss

    (ii)   Recording of business transactions

    (iii)   Preparation of statements for K Ltd's internal use

    (iv)   No legal formats used

141 BB Co has recently reported a profit after tax figure for the year of $880,000. This is prior to preference dividends of $80,000 being deducted. The company has 100,000 shares in issue, 20% of which are preference shares.

The earnings per share (EPS) for the year is $ [   ]

142 Which of the following functions is most likely to be undertaken in a treasury department?

A   Preparation of cash flow statements

B   Foreign currency management

C   Product pricing decisions

D   Key factor analysis

143 An important advantage of using loans to finance investment is:

A   loan interest payments can usually be suspended if profits are low

B   the timing of loan payments is often at the company's discretion

C   loan interest is tax deductible

D   banks will often not require security for loan advances

144 Company G is considering raising finance to invest in new premises. It believes that it should raise debt finance by way of a bank loan.

Which of the following statements is correct regarding debt and equity finance?

A   Interest payments tend to be cheaper than dividends

B   Interest payments can be suspended in the future if H is unable to afford them

C   Dividends are an allowable deduction against H's profits

D   H will likely need to provide asset security to investors whether it chooses to raise debt or equity finance

145 S decided to record the purchases made on the 2nd of April 200X in tax year ending 31st of March 200X. The authorities will likely classify this as tax _____.

Which of the following words correctly fill this gap?

A   Evasion

B   Minimisation

C   Avoidance

D   Suppression

146 Tax mitigation involves which of the following?

A   Taking all legal steps to reduce one's tax liability

B   Agreeing to pay a financial penalty to avoid prosecution

C   Moving businesses and funds offshore to reduce liability to UK tax

D   Reducing tax liabilities without frustrating the law makers' intentions

147 Below are a number of statements regarding internal and external audit.

Which four of the statements relate to internal audit rather than external audit?

A   It is a legal requirement for larger companies

B   The scope of work is decided by management

C   Can be undertaken by employees of the company

D   Ultimately reports to the company's shareholders

E   Reviews whether financial statements are true and fair

F   Must be undertaken by independent auditors

G   Mainly focuses on reviewing internal controls

H   Ultimately reports to management

148 **The key purpose of internal auditing is to:**

A   detect errors and fraud

B   evaluate the organisation's risk management processes and systems of control

C   give confidence as to the truth and fairness of the financial statements

D   express an internal opinion on the truth and fairness of the financial statements

149 **Which of the following specialist roles perform budgets to support the major decisions of the board?**

A   Financial Planning and Analysis

B   Taxation

C   Project Management

D   Project Appraisal

150 **Which of the following specialist roles perform an important role in minimising risk?**

A   Financial Planning and Analysis

B   Taxation

C   Project Management

D   Project Appraisal

151 **Which of the following specialist roles integrate all aspects of a project?**

A   Financial Planning and Analysis

B   Taxation

C   Project Management

D   Project Appraisal

152 Which of the following specialist roles includes providing information on capital investment decisions?

A   Financial Planning and Analysis

B   Taxation

C   Project Management

D   Project Appraisal

153 Are the following statements true or false?

A   Because of the ethical principle of confidentiality, specialists within the organisation cannot work with the finance function.

B   Taxation specialists have a number of key responsibilities including the calculation and interpretation of key financial ratios.

C   Projects can vary in size, resource allocation and complexity.

D   When calculating a payback period today is known as time 0.

154 Which of the following explain recent changes to the specialist areas of an organisation. Select three that apply

A   There are now more opportunities for business partnering between the finance function and the specialist areas.

B   The finance function is no longer a requirement because of advancements in technology.

C   The shape of the finance function is now evolving to a diamond shape.

D   The finance function is constantly improving the shared understanding of how an organisation creates value.

E   "Digital centres of excellence" are now performing the routine management reporting tasks.

155 Complete the following sentence by choosing from the options below

Level two of the diamond shaped finance function involves _____ insight to _____ users. This must be delivered in an appropriate _____ and with appropriate _____.

| Influence | Communicating | Frequency | Marketing | Assertiveness | Format |

156 Working with internal and external stakeholders to influence how the organisation creates and preserves value is known as what?

A   Business process re-engineering

B   Outsourcing the finance function

C   Strategic Business Partnering

D   Smart finance factories

157 Which of the following statements about leadership of the finance team is/are correct?

Statement	True/False?
The CEO is the leader of the finance team.	
The leader of the finance team is responsible for executing and funding strategies.	
The CFO needs a skill set outside of the traditional finance skills.	
Technology has had minimal impact on the leader of the finance function as he/she is so senior in the organisation.	

158 Which of the following two stages in the "information to impact" framework have been most affected by technology and automation?

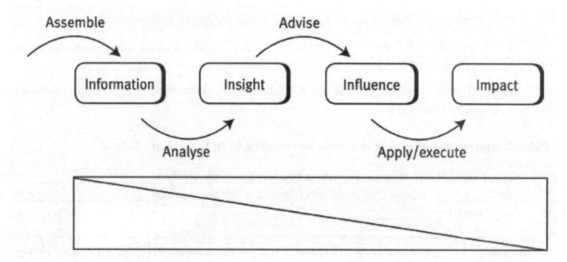

159 Label the following diagram to match the finance activities to the structure of the modern finance function.

Use the following labels

- Data processing

- Managing others

- Stakeholder Interactions

- Data collection

- Applying expertise

160 Artificial intelligence (AI), machine learning and natural language programming are all examples of what?

A Robotic Process Automation

B Data Processing

C Cognitive Computing

D Coding

SYLLABUS SECTION E: FINANCE INTERACTING WITH THE ORGANISATION

161 The range of management issues associated with converting resources into required goods or services within an organisation is known as which one of the following?

A   Sourcing strategies

B   Product marketing

C   Liberalisation

D   Operations management

162 Which one of the following shows the correct sequence in the stages of product/service development?

A   Concept screening, consider customers' needs, design process, time-to-market, product testing.

B   Consider customers' needs, concept screening, design process, time-to-market, product testing.

C   Consider customers' needs, concept screening, design process, product testing, time-to-market.

D   Product testing, time-to-market, consider customers' needs, concept screening, design process.

163 Most supply chains involve which one of the following?

A   A number of different companies

B   An organisation's infrastructure

C   After sales service

D   A strategic apex

164 Loss of goodwill and the expense of product recalls are known as which one of the following?

A   External failure costs

B   Costs of lean

C   Excess production costs

D   Transaction costs

165 A lean approach is associated with which one of the following?

A   Supply sourcing strategies

B   Demographic profiling

C   Employee selection criteria

D   Removal of waste

166 **Which one of the following is not a spoke in Cousins' supply wheel?**

    A   Cost benefit analysis

    B   Portfolio of relationships

    C   Performance measures

    D   A firm's infrastructure

167 **Collaborating with its suppliers may bring a company added value because it can:**

    A   strike a harder bargain with its suppliers

    B   work with a supplier to improve quality and reduce costs

    C   avoid transaction costs

    D   introduce price competition amongst suppliers

168 The emergence of internet selling has increased the need for organisations to focus on their reverse logistics capability.

Is this statement TRUE or FALSE?

    A   True

    B   False

169 **Which three of the following may be advantages of using process maps?**

    A   Highlighting opportunities to standardise processes

    B   Fewer bottlenecks to improve resource utilisation

    C   Visual representation of inefficiencies

    D   Provides an overview of responsibilities

    E   Improves relationships with suppliers

170 **Which one of the following is an example of co-ordination between the finance function and procurement?**

    A   Inventory management

    B   Charge-out rates

    C   Customer service

    D   Creating purchase orders

171 **Which of the following is an example of co-ordination between the finance function and production?**

    A   Establishing credit terms

    B   Advising on prices

    C   Determining sales quantities

    D   Budgeting

172 A computerised system for planning the requirements for raw materials, work-in-progress and finished items is known as what?

    A   ERP

    B   MRP

    C   MRP II

    D   DSS

173 Which of the following is a way in which an organisation's marketing department would co-ordinate with its finance function?

    A   Calculating charge out rates for services provided by the organisation

    B   Calculating the budgets for the number of units to be produced

    C   Estimation of the costs of the raw materials required for production

    D   Decisions on the quality of raw materials that the organisation can afford to use

174 E Co has a large marketing department. In which of the following ways would this department co-ordinate with E's finance function?

    A   Decisions on the quantity of raw materials required

    B   Establishing credit terms for customers

    C   Calculating pay rises for staff

    D   Decisions on the selling price of the product

175 Which of the following market research data-gathering techniques is most likely to be effective in estimating how many people buy a consumer product, in what quantities and how often?

    A   Sample surveys

    B   Observation

    C   Analysis of past sales for consumer products in total

    D   Group interviewing

176 An organisational approach that involves targeting an entire market with a single marketing mix is known as which one of the following?

    A   Undifferentiated

    B   Differentiated

    C   Saturated

    D   Blanket

177 **Match the forms of marketing communication in the list below to the correct definitions.**

- Viral
- Guerrilla
- Experiential
- Digital

Term	Definition
	An interactive marketing experience aimed at stimulating all the senses.
	The promotion of products or brands via one or more forms of electronic media.
	Relies on well thought out, highly focused and often unconventional attacks on key targets.
	Encourages individuals to pass on a marketing message to others, so creating exponential growth in the message's exposure.

178 Molly is currently assessing the use of intermediaries needed to get her product to the end consumers.

Which part of the marketing mix is she assessing?

A   Product

B   Price

C   Place

D   Promotion

179 **The pricing policy which involves setting a low price to gain market share is known as what?**

A   Price skimming

B   Penetration pricing

C   Price discrimination

D   Loss leaders

180 Which two of the following statements are true regarding technology and market research?

A   Organisations can conduct focus groups online through technology allowing them to interact with people across wide geographic boundaries

B   All data held online is valid

C   Due to the volume of data it now takes longer to gain business insight

D   Click analysis is a tool used to track the actions of individual users within a website

181 Label the diagram of the product life cycle using some of the options below.

Options

- Cash
- Revenue
- Time
- Maturity
- Introduction
- Peak
- Trough
- Decline
- Growth
- Innovation

182 Match the pricing policy to its correct description

Pricing policy	Description
Price discrimination	Setting a high initial price when a product is new
Going rate pricing	Altering prices in line with demand
Penetration pricing	Charging a different price for the same product to a different market segment
Price skimming	Setting a low price to gain market share
Dynamic pricing	Matching competitors prices

183 Dividing the market into groups of homogenous people is otherwise known as what in the context of marketing?

A   Situation analysis

B   Positioning

C   Targeting

D   Segmentation

184 Khilan is monitoring transport and storage costs as KPIs for sales and marketing.

Which element of the marketing mix is he focussing on specifically?

A   Product

B   Price

C   Place

D   Promotion

185 Personal characteristics, qualifications and necessary experience expected of a particular post holder are normally all found in which one of the following documents?

A   Job description

B   Person specification

C   Reference letter

D   Summary appraisal meeting record

186 **Match the stage of the HR cycle below with the correct description.**

- Appraisal

- Training

- Development

- Selection

Stage	Description
	Choosing the best person for the job from a field of candidates sourced via recruitment.
	Systematic review and assessment of an employee's performance, potential and training needs.
	Formal learning to achieve the level of skills, knowledge and competence to carry out the current role.
	Realisation of a person's potential through formal and informal learning to enable them to carry out their current and future role.

187 Andrea has just attended her appraisal with her line manager. She felt that the feedback was poorly delivered and that the manager viewed it purely as a form filling exercise.

Which two of Lockett's barriers to effective appraisal may have been present here?

A Chat, bureaucracy

B Confrontation, unfinished business

C Chat, judgement

D Confrontation, bureaucracy

188 **An effective appraisal system involves:**

A assessing the personality of the appraisee

B a process initiated by the manager who needs an update from the appraisee

C advising on the faults of the appraise

D a participative, problem-solving process between the manager and appraise

189 **Which HR activity could be monitored using the KPIs of employee absenteeism and productivity?**

A Reward systems

B Performance management

C Training and Development

D Motivation

190   True or false, the psychological contract is a legally binding document that exists between an employer and an employee?

191   Match the type of flexible working arrangement to the correct explanation.

Type of flexible working arrangement	Explanation
Remote working/ teleworking	Working outside of normal working day patterns
Flexitime	Fewer hours than the standard weekly number
Shift system	Standard hours within fewer days in a shift rotation
Compressed week	The need to work a standard set of hours but less restriction on when these hours are worked
Job sharing	Technology has enabled employees to work away from the office, usually at home
Part-time	Two employees share a standard hour week

192   Which of the following is not an advantage of individual performance related pay?

A   Encourages teamwork

B   Employee controllability

C   Goal congruence

D   Motivation

193   Complete the following sentences from the words below.

Traditionally the HR function and the finance function worked _____.

People were regarded by finance as _____. Nowadays people are regarded as _____.

- assets
- independently
- collaboratively
- costs
- liabilities

194 Match the HR activity to the most appropriate KPI

Activity	KPI
Recruitment and Selection	Turnover rate
Training and Development	Competitiveness of salary
Performance management	Delegate feedback scores
Motivation	Female to male ratio
Reward system	Appraisals completed on time

195 The "systematic review and assessment of an employee's performance, potential and training needs" describes what?

A   Training

B   Development

C   Appraisal

D   Induction

196 Alexander is reviewing a graph which is giving him an overview of the monthly performance of his team. He notices one team member is underperforming and wishes to know more details. The system lets Alexander drill down to get further details.

What type of system is Alexander using?

A   Decision support system

B   Expert system

C   Knowledge management system

D   Executive information system

197 What sort of system could be used to obtain specialist tax knowledge?

A   Decision support system

B   Expert system

C   Knowledge management system

D   Executive information system

198 What is the type of knowledge that is held by people and has not been formally documented?

A   Explicit knowledge

B   Informal knowledge

C   Human knowledge

D   Tacit knowledge

199 **Which three of the following are advantages of remote working for the organisation?**

A   Increased control over staff

B   Reduced absenteeism

C   Reduced labour costs

D   Reduced infrastructure costs

E   Increased employee motivation

200 **Groupware, the intranet, and extranets are examples of what type of systems?**

A   Decision support systems

B   Expert systems

C   Knowledge management systems

D   Appraisal system

201 P Co is an organisation which outsources most of its functions and exists primarily as a network of contracts.

What type of organisation is P Co?

A   Virtual organisation

B   Modular organisation

C   Matrix organisation

D   Remote organisation

202 **Linda works as part of a virtual team, which three of the following challenges is she likely to face?**

A   Sharing information with other members of her team

B   Feelings of isolation

C   Over supervision from her line manager

D   Cultural differences

E   Lack of delegation

203 Paul has been given the task of ensuring his organisation goes beyond compliance with technology and data legislation.

What is this commitment known as?

A   Ethics

B   Corporate social responsibility

C   Corporate digital responsibility

D   Sustainability

204 **Which of the following is not a benefit of big data analytics**

A   Improved decision making

B   Market customisation

C   Increased security of data

D   Product innovation

205 **The movement of data through a process or system is also known as what?**

A   Data flow

B   Data outputs

C   Data warehousing

D   Data mining

206 Steele Co are choosing between centralised and decentralised IS architecture.

Which approach will give them greater control over there information systems?

A   Centralised

B   Decentralised

207 Raj has been analysing trends in the online reviews on social media for his organisation's main product line. However, he has noticed many inconsistencies.

Which of the 4 Vs of big data may be causing this problem?

A   Volume

B   Variety

C   Velocity

D   Veracity

Section 2

ANSWERS TO OBJECTIVE TEST QUESTIONS

SYLLABUS SECTION A: ROLE OF THE FINANCE FUNCTION

1   **C**

Staffing numbers is part of resource allocation – an important role of the finance function will be working out which resources the organisation will require to achieve its objectives.

2   **B, E, F**

Quantitative measures are numerical, whereas, qualitative performance measure are non-numerical. Sales, profit and number of units produced are all numerical measures of performance.

3

Completing work carefully, thoroughly and diligently, in accordance with relevant technical and professional standards.	Professional competence and due care
Being straightforward, honest and truthful in all professional and business relationships.	Integrity
Non-disclosure of information unless you have specific permission or a legal or professional duty to do so.	Confidentiality
Not allowing bias, conflict of interest, or the influence of other people to override your professional judgement.	Objectivity
Compliance with relevant laws and regulations.	Professional behaviour

4   **C**

Professional competence and due care. If Polly undertakes the work knowing that she will not be able to complete it to the best of her ability she would not be behaving with due care.

5   B

Confidentiality. Gemma must not share information unless she has specific permission or a legal duty to do so.

6   A, B, E

The reputation of a business can be enhanced if they behave in an ethical manner, this can also attract employees and new customers to increase revenue.

It may increase costs, however, this would not be a benefit.

Risk should actually reduce for a more ethical business, not increase.

7   D, E, F

Connected stakeholders have a transaction with the business, such as suppliers, customers and lenders. Employees are internal stakeholders, whilst the government and environmental pressure groups are external stakeholders.

8   A, B, D

Increased costs is an argument against the introduction of CSR principles. One of the criticisms of CSR is that businesses may just use it as a PR exercise.

9   TRUE

By definition

10   B, C, E

Increased contact with shareholders is an indication of good corporate governance.

An emphasis on short term profitability would be an indicator of poor governance not long term.

11   D

By definition

12   A

Answers B and D relate to 'enables' and answer C relates to 'narrates how'.

13   A, B, F

The nominations committee oversees appointments to the board. The remuneration committee oversees the pay of the executive directors. The audit committee acts as a liaison between the directors and the auditors.

14   D

The positions of the Chairman (the person who runs the board) and the CEO (the person in charge of running the company) should be separated. This is to ensure that no one individual has too much power within the company.

15   **B**

To be considered as an independent NED, an individual must not have been an employee of the company in the last five years.

16   **D**

The nominations committee ensures that all appointments are based on merit and suitability and that the composition of the board is balanced.

17   **C**

Traditionalists do not believe in CSR and have the opinion that a business should not exceed its obligations for stakeholders.

18   **A**

Internal stakeholders are those within the business, for example employees.

Connected stakeholders are those who have a transaction with the business, for example customers and suppliers.

External stakeholders are those outside of the business, for example the general public.

19

Stakeholder	Need/expectation
Employees	Pay, working conditions and job security
Shareholders	Dividends and capital growth
Government	Provision of taxes and jobs and compliance with legislation
Customers	Value-for-money products and services

20   **D**

The chairman runs the board, not the company. The person in charge of running the company is the chief executive officer not the chief economic officer.

21

The preparation of forecasts, for example of future sales or material prices, will be an important role of the finance function in enabling the organisation to create and preserve value.

The preparation of comprehensive reports for shareholders will be an important role of the finance function in narrating how the organisation creates and preserves value.

The preparation of variance analysis for control purposes will be an important role of the finance function in shaping how the organisation creates and preserves value.

22   **A**

Schools is the correct answer because the other organisations are normally found in the private (i.e. non-governmental) sector.

23   D

Both these statements are false. It would be unwise to assume fixed IFRS rules in a changing environment. Equally the finance function should attempt to anticipate potential changes and be ready to respond.

24   C

The sacking of someone for gross misconduct is not in itself poor CSR, the employee may well have deserved the treatment. Products often have known failure rates (light bulbs) and as long as false claims are not made this is not necessarily poor CSR. Redundancy is sometimes necessary to save the company and the jobs of the majority.

25   C

All the examples contain an agency relationship of some sort, but C is the generally accepted definition of agency risk.

26   FALSE

Not-for-profit organisations will also be affected by rapid changes in technology. The finance function will need to adapt in these types of entities just as much as within profit seeking entities.

27   C and D are true

Whilst change may bring about risk (A) is can also present opportunities.

Despite change being unpredictable (B), organisations still have to plan for different ways of doing business.

All businesses will be affected in some way, even the smallest businesses.

28   C

The information is taking 14 hours to gather which will cost money. If it is immediately being filed, the benefit will be less than this cost.

29   E

The fifth A is Analyse not Align.

30   C

Assembling information involves collecting data from a range of sources.

31   TRUE

By definition

32   B

Analyse : for insights could take the form of comparing actual to budget. This activity can also be viewed as the broad role of questioning.

33   A, B and D

The data can have relevance to the organisation (answer C) although it may not meet the exact needs of the business.

It is not unethical to use external data as long as the data has been gathered in an ethical manner.

34   B

By definition

35   A, B and E

These are all examples of internal sources of data. Newspaper articles and exchange rate information would be gathered from external sources.

36   D

This can be seen on the below diagram.

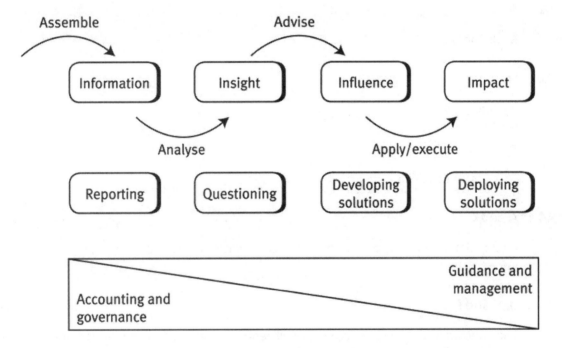

37   A

Information which contains typos or casting errors is not accurate.

38   B

Providing insight to users by analysing information can take the form of a comparison of the information with the budgeted or historical figures.

39   C

Sales growth of 20% may not be significant if it is put into context, for example if the industry is growing by 35% (answer A).

Non-financial data can sometimes be quantified, it can still be expressed in numerical terms, for example number of complaints (answer B).

Good quality analysis does rely on a representative sample of the population (answer C).

Number of training days is non-financial, not non-quantifiable. It can be counted (answer D).

40   D

Finance professionals apply the information to harness value for the organisation through their impact. This activity can also be viewed as the broad role of deploying solutions.

SYLLABUS SECTION B: TECHNOLOGY IN A DIGITAL WORLD

41   B

By definition

42   D

By definition

43   A

This describes the basic idea of cloud computing.

44   A and C

Public clouds are hosted by 3rd parties. Private clouds are managed over a private infrastructure.

45   B, C and D

The contract with the cloud provider will require careful management, this also increases reliance on the 3rd party and can result in job losses in IT support and maintenance roles.

Scalability, increased flexibility and reduced cost are all advantages of cloud computing.

46   B, C and E

Option A is incorrect in that big data does not refer to any specific financial amount. Option D is also incorrect. Big data can indeed come from many sources, but this is too narrow a definition. Big data refers to the large volume of data, the many sources of data and the many types of data.

47

A	National Statistics – **Open**	
B	Social media posts – **Human Sourced**	
C	Emails – **Human Sourced**	
D	Smart meters – **Machine Generated**	
E	Customer database – **Processed**	
F	Census – **Open**	
G	Home assistants – **Machine Generated**	
H	Fixed asset register – **Processed**	

48   C

Increasingly process automation is focussing on more complex business areas which can save costs and enable employees to focus on more value adding activities.

49   C

This is a description of artificial intelligence.

50   A

By definition

51   A, B and D

In order to increase security and address the issue of cyber risk, all of the transactions in a blockchain are publically available and all transactions must be verified by a decentralised network of computers.

52   D

By definition. Answer C is too narrow an explanation although is an example of the use of the Internet of Things. Answer B is the definition of blockchain.

53   TRUE

News is now consumed via mobile devices and is live rather than being a record of yesterday's news.

54   B

By definition

55   C

This best describes the process of 3-D printing.

56   A, C and D

Traditional industries such as banking and the news have now been replaced by online versions and apps. Music is also now being downloaded or streamed instantly.

Social media interactions (B) have increased, and the costs have declined for manufacturers as the technologies develop (E).

57   B, D and E

A is incorrect as 3-D printing does not involve batch production (traditional manufacture which is more focused on large volumes of identical products).

C is incorrect as there are no off-cuts with 3-D printing. 3D printing sees the exact design printed and nothing else.

58   A, B and C

Cloud technology allows pay as you go computing charged based on what a company actually needs and is therefore cost efficient.

Cloud computing allows frequent upgrades making it scalable.

Cloud computing supports remote working increasing flexibility.

59   D

By definition. Veracity considers the reliability of the data being received.

60   A

The most common use of data visualisation is in creating a dashboard to display the key performance indicators of a business in a live format, thus allowing immediate understanding of current performance.

B is incorrect as the data is displayed in customisable formats.

Data visualisation has nothing to do with virtual reality (answer C).

D is incorrect as a core element of data visualisation is understanding and ease of use, hence removing the need for IT professionals.

61   A

These technologies which are considered to be main stream are termed core modernisation tools, examples include the cloud.

62   B

These technologies are still at the early adopter stage and are termed exponentials, examples include blockchain.

63   B

Many cloud services are provided by external third parties, and therefore reliance on these suppliers will be increased.

64   FALSE

Multiple users can collaborate at the same time but cloud computing reduces the risk of version control issues.

65   A, D and E

Training will still be required for staff to understand how the new software works and interfaces with their roles.

Process automation changes the way the finance function works and can lead to uncertainty around job security and future prospects, there will not necessarily be automatic buy in by the staff.

66   D

By definition

67   A

The graphic produced will only be as accurate as the original data. Visualisation does not improve this accuracy.

68   B

Statements (i) and (iii) are true.

Statement (ii) is false because there is no agreement yet as to how these assets should be accounted for.

Statement (iv) is incorrect as cross border payments should be made much simpler through the use of blockchain.

69   A

The impact of 3-D printing on the finance function is largely from a costing perspective, practically dealing with the changes in operations this technology allows.

70   A, C and D

The remaining two qualities are 'give up control yet architect the choices' and 'rely on data yet trust your intuition'.

71   B

The intangible assets of the company such as a network of contacts are internally generated and therefore cannot be recognised on the statement of financial position, this may understate their true value.

72   B

The new technology is driving an expansion beyond sample-based testing to include analysis of entire populations of audit-relevant data, using intelligent analytics to deliver a higher quality of audit evidence and more relevant business insights.

Whilst statement D is correct, it has more relevance to the management accounting function than internal audit.

Statements A and C are false.

73   FALSE

Accounting for cryptocurrency is currently a grey area for standard setters and exactly how they should be classified is subject to ongoing debate.

74   D

Use of mobile technology has reduced duplication and data entry. App software for logging and recording expenses has reduced manual processing, whilst delivering significant efficiencies and better quality management information.

75   C

Judgement involves making decisions, evaluating data sources and applying knowledge to make sound judgements.

76   A

This describes business acumen.

77   B, C and D

GDPR requires data to be kept for no longer than is necessary, it does not suggest a number of years.

78   FALSE

Compliance with legislation such as the GDPR laws is something that all companies should achieve. However, there are also ethical considerations as to what companies do and how they act.

79   A and C

CDR goes beyond mere compliance and is a voluntary commitment which will improve the risk management of the business.

80   C

Digital inclusion sees businesses share data in a benevolent way to other causes or organisations that may benefit from their data assets.

SYLLABUS SECTION C: DATA AND INFORMATION IN A DIGITAL WORLD

81

Jane – operational

Bill – strategic

Colleen – tactical

82   FALSE

Whilst the statement about enhancing competitive advantage is true, valuable information can also offer significant cost savings through improvements to operational efficiencies.

83   A, B and E

C and D are ways that data and technology can support the operations function, rather than marketing.

84   A, B and C

D is how data and technology can support the HR function.

E is how data and technology can support the marketing function.

85   D

Digital assets are assets held by a business in digital form that do not have physical substance.

86   B

The videos would be an example of a digital asset.

87   C and D

The access is both in a single central location and only allowed with the correct authorisation, making A and B incorrect.

88   FALSE

Version control, watermarking and embargo dates allow increased security and protect assets from improper use. Additionally, access levels built into the system allow access only to those with authorisation.

89   D

Tactical decisions are medium term and involve putting the strategic plan into action.

90   C

A digital asset management system is designed to coordinate the digital assets of a business, ensuring they are held centrally in an accessible, secure and logically designed repository.

91   C

The three decision making systems support each other. Operational errors might well cause cost overruns.

92   B

The sales invoice total is data only. The lead time information is not relevant to the sales director and the price list is again just data without analysis.

93   D

A staggering number!

94   B

Admittedly the technology makes data gathering more efficient and quicker but the nature of the data is also changing, with more information than was previously available being gathered. For example, a customer may have considered an alternative before buying, in the past this fact would be lost. Short lead times enable business to respond to the signals and trend that data is revealing.

95   D

Permission cannot be shared and increasingly digital assets are protected. Embargo dates can be used to withdraw permissions after a certain time.

96   D

By definition

Answers A and C are strategic decisions whilst B describes operational decision making.

97   A

Decisions about mergers and acquisitions happen at the strategic level.

98   D

Data can enable new market segments to be identified, which may previously have been lost within a broader market segment.

99   D

Data from past product launches and company promotions for an entire industry combined with the subsequent sales performance of those products provides huge insight into what promotions work best and when. This can reduce the guesswork by supporting companies with real data.

100 B

Deviations from expected performance give early warning of potential problems and preventative maintenance can be scheduled at a convenient time and before an asset breaks down.

101 A

The sales function would require live data on competitors' pricing and market trends to enable them to set selling prices.

102 C

The HR function requires data to incorporate appraisal systems, productivity analysis as well as collecting data on internal progressions and training days.

103 D

A move to integrated reporting to the shareholders could see a shift in data needs and reporting. For instance data about carbon footprint and water usage.

104 A

The directors seek insight and clarity form information provided by finance, this is often required in the form of data visualisation.

105 C

Extraction, transformation, loading

106

Level	Description
Conceptual	Business oriented and practical, considering the business data and its requirements
Logical	This level begins to develop a technical map of rules and data structures defining how data will be held and used
Physical	This considers how the defined system requirements will be implemented using a specific database management system

107 B

By definition

108 B

By definition

109 D

The constant stream of data being produced in real time, is referred to as the velocity of big data.

110 A

This describes business intelligence.

111 D

ETL stands for extraction, transformation and loading. The ETL system is a single tool combining the processes of extraction (answer A), transformation (answer B) and loading (answer C).

112 A

Data visualisation is an enabling technology that complements data analytics by facilitating user friendly and accessible presentation of key data.

113 B

Veracity relates to the extent that the data can be relied upon. Systems must ensure data can be validated to reduce uncertainty to tolerable levels.

114 C

Productive efficiency is not an issue for either the external auditors or customers. Shareholders will care about productivity insofar as it translates to profit and dividend but not on an individual level. Internal auditors are focussed on value for money (VFM) and efficiency is part of that.

115 D

Whilst the directors will be looking at this data, they're doing so wondering what a lender will make of the figures. Shareholders might also be interested but again it is the lenders that are more concerned about these metrics.

116 D

Too much data is possible. It could be too expensive to calculate, too detailed or overly confusing. An average, whilst potentially useful, is unlikely to be enough to manage the business.

117 C

By definition

The data strategy should establish clear, consistent user friendly policies on the use and storage of data to ensure correct use and minimise risk of data breaches.

118 B

Structural is not a level in a data modelling process. The three levels of a data modelling process are conceptual, logical and physical.

119 D

The order is wrong in both these statements. Data is profiled, then extracted, transformed and loaded in to a data warehouse.

120 B, C and E

The detail described in answer A is too detailed for the infographic. Access will not necessarily be suitable for all sales staff as described in answer D.

SYLLABUS SECTION D: SHAPE AND STRUCTURE OF THE FINANCE FUNCTION

121 B

Because the entrepreneurial structure is run by one person who makes all the decisions, this powerful individual will have strong control over the organisation and its strategic direction, leading to better goal congruence.

122 D

Function managers may make decisions to increase their own power, or in the interests of their own function, rather than in the interests of the company overall. Economies of scale, standardisation and specialists feeling comfortable are advantages of a functional structure.

123 D

A refers to an entrepreneurial structure.

B is typical of a functional structure.

C describes a divisional structure.

In a matrix structure individuals will have dual command, a functional manager and a divisional manager. This can cause conflict between departments and stress for the individual.

124 C and D

The first two features relate to a functional structure.

125 A

If H wants to manage each product separately, it will need to adopt either a matrix or divisional approach, as these would allow the creation of separate divisions for each product. However, H wishes to keep its administrative costs as low as possible. As the matrix structure has high admin costs due to high numbers of managers, A should adopt a divisional approach.

126 D

The granting of authority over each divisional geographic area to geographic bosses results in a potential loss of control over key operating decisions. This weakness is also present in the product divisional structure.

127 A

The span of control is the number of people for whom a manager is directly responsible.

Scalar chain relates to the number of management levels within an organisation.

128

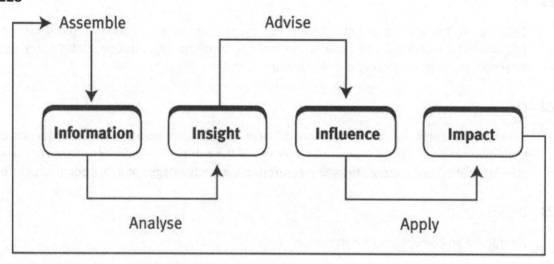

129 A

Assembling information can be viewed as the broad role of reporting where there is an emphasis on accounting and governance (for example, financial reporting, management accounting, regulatory compliance, risk management and corporate governance).

130 **Technology and automation** will play an important role in all of the activities of the finance function but will have the largest impact on the '**assembly**' and '**analysis**' activities.

This will 'free up' the resource of the finance function professionals who can now place greater focus on the '**advising**' and '**applying/executing**' activities.

131

132

Statement	True?
An advantage of outsourcing is reduced headcount and therefore reduced cost	✓
Outsourcing can enable an organisation to access expertise that it might otherwise be lacking	✓
A drawback of outsourcing is that it distracts management and they lose focus of their core activities	This is false. In fact, outsourcing should enable management to focus on their core activities as it removes a distraction
Transaction costs are a benefit to the business	Transaction costs are an expense not a benefit
Outsourcing may lead to redundancies which can affect employee morale	✓

133   A, B, D

Shared service centres provide the opportunity to standardise processes, which makes control easier and allows for consistent reporting.

Advancements in technology are not a benefit of shared service centres but rather has facilitated their development.

A shared service centre is often established in a multinational organisation which has operations in several countries. The complexities of these countries including different laws, taxes, languages, cultures and reporting requirements may make this difficult.

134 A

When outsourcing, transaction costs arise from the effort that must be put into specifying what is required and subsequently co-ordinating delivery and monitoring quality.

135

One of the main activities of the finance function is 'advising to influence'. Broadly speaking this can be referred to as DEVELOPING SOLUTIONS. It involves the finance function communicating insights to influence decision making.

136 BPR

Business Process Re-engineering

RPA stands for Robotic Process Automation , TQM means Total Quality Management, and Kaizen is a philosophy of continual improvement.

137 C

The strategic level of the finance function is more likely to focus on information for external stakeholders.

138 A

The treasury department will monitor foreign exchange and try to minimise the company's exposure to foreign exchange losses.

139 D

The other three are correct for financial accounting.

140 (i)   B

(ii)   B

(iii)   A

(iv)   A

141 10

EPS   = PAT less pref divs/weighted average number of ordinary shares in issue.

= $880,000 - $80,000/100,000 \times 80\%$

= \$10

142 B

While treasurers will deal with cash management (amongst other things) they do not produce cash flow statements – this is part of the role of a financial accounting function. C and D would both be undertaken by a management accountant.

143 C

A, B and D are not true. They describe advantages of using the issue of share capital to finance investment.

144 A

Interest tends to be cheaper than dividends. However, a company cannot normally suspend debt repayments if it can no longer afford them – this is only possible with dividends. Dividends are not an allowable deduction, but interest is. Finally, shareholders would not normally receive any security on their investment, meaning that D is also incorrect.

145 A

This is tax evasion as the company is illegally reducing its tax liability. Note that it cannot be both evasion and avoidance simultaneously.

146 D

Tax avoidance is used to describe schemes which, whilst they are legal, are designed to defeat the intentions of the law makers. Thus, once a tax avoidance scheme becomes public knowledge, the law makers will usually step in to change the law to stop the scheme from working.

147 B, C, G and H

148 B

The internal audit also makes recommendations for the achievement of company objectives. C is the role of the external auditors.

149 A

Financial Planning and Analysis (FP&A) specialists play a crucial role in organisations by performing budgeting, forecasting and data analysis that supports the major organisational decisions of the board.

150 B

Taxation specialists minimise risk by focusing on two main areas: tax compliance and tax planning.

151 C

Project management is the integration of all aspects of a project, ensuring that the proper knowledge and resources are available when and where needed, and above all to ensure the expected outcome is produced in a timely, cost effective manner.

152 D

Project appraisal will take place prior to a project commencing, one of the most important decisions will involve capital investment.

153 A – FALSE. The finance function works alongside these specialists providing expert support for decisions and projects and helps to formulate strategies so that the business is able to adapt to the ever changing environment.

B – FALSE. This is the responsibility of Financial Planning and Analysis.

C – TRUE. All projects are different and it is the role of the project management to integrate all aspects of it.

D – TRUE. Today is known as time 0 in project appraisal.

154 A, C and D are the correct answers

B is incorrect because technology improves the productivity of the finance function, it is still a vital function within an organisation.

E is incorrect because the digital centres of excellence provide further insight into value creation. They are not performing routine tasks.

155 Level two of the diamond shaped finance function involves **communicating** insight to **influence** users. This must be delivered in an appropriate **format**, and with appropriate **frequency**.

156 C

Strategic Business Partnering sees the finance function acting as a business partner **influencing** the organisation's decisions to achieve the desired organisational **impact**.

157

Statement	True/False?
The CEO is the leader of the finance team.	False, the leader of the finance team is the CFO (Chief Financial Officer).
The leader of the finance team is responsible for executing and funding strategies.	True, it is their responsibility to lead the finance team to achieve the desired organisational impact including the executing and funding of strategies set out by the CEO.
The CFO needs a skill set outside of the traditional finance skills.	True, the CFO requires skills such as regulation, risk management, business transformation, supply chain management and IT.
Technology has had minimal impact on the leader of the finance function as he/she is so senior in the organisation.	False, The CFO is increasingly relying on automation of key business processes and is relying more on technology to transform data into actionable insights that can influence and impact the organisation's achievement of its goals.

158 Assembly and Analysis

Technology and automation will play an important role in all of the activities of the finance function but will have the largest impact on the 'assembly' and 'analysis' activities.

159

160 C

The term cognitive computing has been used to refer to new hardware and/or software that mimics the functioning of the human brain.

SYLLABUS SECTION E: FINANCE INTERACTING WITH THE ORGANISATION

161 D

By definition

162 B

The correct sequence in the stages of product/ service development is consider customers' needs, concept screening, design process, time-to-market, product testing.

163 A

Most companies outsource at least part of their supply chain.

164 A

By definition

165 D

Lean management is a philosophy that aims to systematically reduce waste.

166 D

Cousins' strategic supply wheel is made up of five spokes; organisation structure, relationships with suppliers, cost/benefit, competences and performance measures.

167 B

It is now recognised that successful management of suppliers is based upon collaboration. A company should be able to improve quality and reduce costs as a result of this collaboration.

168 A – TRUE

Internet selling has increased the average level of returns received by an organisation and has resulted in an increased focus on their reverse logistics capability in order to reduce costs, improve customer service and increase revenue.

169 A, C and D

B and E are benefits of improved supply chain management.

170 A

Purchasing will consult with the inventory section of the finance function to determine the quantity of items already in stock and therefore the quantity required.

171 D

Production will decide how many items of what type are to be produced. The cost of producing these will be determined by the finance function and production together, and incorporated into the overall budget.

172 B

Material Requirement Planning (MRP). This system is designed to answer what is needed, how much is needed and when is it needed.

173 A

Option A would most likely be a marketing or service provision crossover with the finance function. The other options relate to co-ordination between the production department and the finance function.

174 D

The finance function can help ensure a profitable selling price is used for E's products.

175 A

An analysis of past sales (answer C) will provide information about total sales, but not about how many customers buy the product, nor in what quantities or how frequently. Observation (answer B) is useful for looking at a customer's buying habits, but does not provide information about the numbers of customers for a product or the frequency of buying. Group interviews (answer D) can be useful for obtaining information about customer attitudes/consumer attitudes, but the group size is fairly small and so cannot provide reliable estimates of sales measurements.

Sample surveys (answer A) in different geographical areas are likely to provide reasonably reliable information about numbers of customers, buying quantities and buying frequency.

176 A

By definition

177

Term	Definition
Viral	Encourages individuals to pass on a marketing message to others, so creating exponential growth in the message's exposure.
Guerrilla	Relies on well thought out, highly focused and often unconventional attacks on key targets.
Experiential	An interactive marketing experience aimed at stimulating all the senses.
Digital	The promotion of products or brands via one or more forms of electronic media.

178 C

Place within the marketing mix includes the use of intermediaries, as well as distribution channels, transportation and storage.

179 B

By definition

180 A and D

B is not correct, just because the data is held online does not automatically mean that it is valid.

C is not correct, business insight can be gained faster and more comprehensively than before.

181

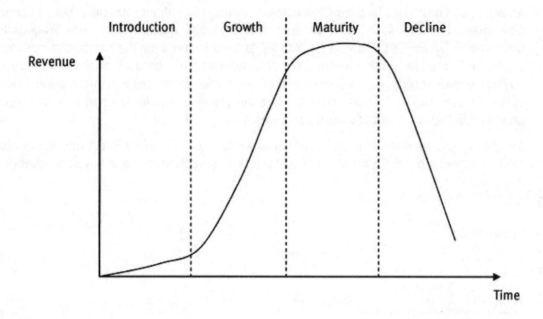

182

Pricing policy	Description
Price discrimination	Charging a different price for the same product to a different market segment
Going rate pricing	Matching competitors prices
Penetration pricing	Setting a low price to gain market share
Price skimming	Setting a high initial price when a product is new
Dynamic pricing	Altering prices in line with demand

183 D

Market segmentation is the process of sub-dividing the market into homogenous groups to whom a separate marketing mix can be focused.

184 C

Place includes distribution of the product which also includes transportation and storage.

185 B

By definition

186

Stage	Description
Selection	Choosing the best person for the job from a field of candidates sourced via recruitment.
Appraisal	Systematic review and assessment of an employee's performance, potential and training needs.
Training	Formal learning to achieve the level of skills, knowledge and competence to carry out the current role.
Development	Realisation of a person's potential through formal and informal learning to enable them to carry out their current and future role.

187 D

Feedback being poorly delivered is an example of confrontation. The manager viewing appraisal as purely a form filling exercise is an example of bureaucracy.

188 D

A key word in the question is 'effective'. Effective appraisal requires a dialogue between the manager and the person being appraised (the 'appraisee'). Any problems with the appraisee's work or performance are identified and should be discussed and resolved constructively. Answer C, in contrast, describes an ineffective appraisal process.

189 D

Low rates of employee absenteeism and high productivity can indicate a high level of motivation of the workforce.

190 FALSE

Unlike the employment contract, the psychological contract is highly subjective, not written down and not legally binding.

191

Type of flexible working arrangement	Explanation
Remote working/teleworking	Technology has enabled employees to work away from the office, usually at home
Flexitime	The need to work a standard set of hours but less restriction on when these hours are worked
Shift system	Working outside of normal working day patterns
Compressed week	Standard hours within fewer days in a shift rotation
Job sharing	Two employees share a standard hour week
Part-time	Fewer hours than the standard weekly number

192 A

Individual performance related pay can sometimes result in a lack of team work as individuals may pursue their own goals at the expense of others.

193

Traditionally the HR function and the finance function worked **independently**.

People were regarded by finance as **costs**. Nowadays people are regarded as **assets**.

194

Activity	KPI
Recruitment and Selection	Female to male ratio
Training and Development	Delegate feedback scores
Performance management	Appraisals completed on time
Motivation	Turnover rate
Reward system	Competitiveness of salary

195 C

By definition

196 D

An executive information system (EIS) gives senior management access to internal and external information. Information is presented in a flexible, user-friendly, summarised form with the option to 'drill down' to a greater level of detail.

197 B

Expert systems hold specialist knowledge to allow non-experts to interrogate them for information.

198 D

Tacit knowledge is personal knowledge and expertise held by people within the organisation that has not been formally documented, for example knowledge gained through the experiences of employees within the organisation.

199 B, D and E

Control over staff will be reduced. Labour costs may actually increase for example, providing employees with equipment.

200 C

These are examples of technology that can assist in knowledge management.

201 A

A virtual organisation is one which outsources most or all of its functions to other organisations and simply exists as a network of contracts, with very few, if any, functions being kept in-house.

202 A, B and D

Knowledge sharing may prove more difficult due to the absence of face to face contact.

Some team members may find this way of working isolating.

Team members will be from different backgrounds and cultural differences may make working together more difficult.

203 C

Corporate Digital Responsibility (CDR) is a voluntary commitment by organisations to go beyond mere compliance with legislation, when it comes to how they handle technology and data.

204 C

The security of data is a major concern in the majority of organisations and if the organisation lacks the resources to manage data then there is likely to be a greater risk of leaks and losses.

205 A

Data flow is the movement of data through a process or system. It includes data inputs, data processing and data outputs.

206 A

Centralisation often leads to greater control at a central level, enabling greater goal congruence.

207 D

Veracity refers to the reliability of the data being analysed. Often online reviews are difficult to rely upon.